MEDICALESE

A Humorous Medical Dictionary

Laugh for Health!

by **Peter Meyer**, MD

**illustrated by
Steve Likens**

Avian-Cetacean Press

Printed and bound in the United States of America. Published by Avian-Cetacean Press in Wilmington, NC.

All pen-and-ink illustrations, except on page 35, are by master cartoonist Steve Likens. The illustration on page 35 and all photographs are by the author.

Comments, suggestions and humorous material for possible inclusion in subsequent editions of *Medicalese* are welcome: Send communications to the author, c/o Avian-Cetacean Press, PO Box 4532, Wilmington, NC 28406.

10 9 8 7 6 5 4 3 2 1

Library of Congress Catalog Card Number: 93-74044

ISBN: 0-9628186-1-5

Dedication

Medicalese is dedicated to health professionals
everywhere who truly care.

The practice of medicine is increasingly demanding. The ominous threat of malpractice, increasing dependence on technology, erosion of personal relationships between caregivers and patients, growing paperwork, burgeoning regulations, and finally, the loss of medical control to administrators, government, insurance companies, and HMOs, all serve to make the practice of modern-day medicine more difficult.

Despite these impediments, the great majority of medical personnel remain dedicated to their responsibilities: Patient care continues to be foremost in their minds. *Medicalese* is dedicated to those professionals, the ones who truly care.

Author's Note and Disclaimer

I trust and hope that *Medicalese* will be taken in the humorous vein in which it is intended. Subjects such as the AMA, hospital administrators, surgeons, and ward clerks are lampooned in *Medicalese*. In actuality, these organizations and individuals provide valuable and sincere care to patients. Thus, under no circumstances should the contents of this book be taken seriously.

I apologize for material in *Medicalese* which readers find offensive or sexist. Professionalism is important in medicine. Treating patients to the very best of our abilities is the goal of myself and many fine medical caregivers with whom I have worked.

Yet, humor is important in medicine (indeed, in *any* field). Laughing at the idiosyncrasies and foibles of patients *and* ourselves helps us deal more positively and effectively with patients. I do not seek to belittle or denigrate patients, caregivers, or the art of medicine with this book. Rather, I hope to make patients and medical personnel laugh, and thereby to relieve their anxieties, frustrations, and fears.

Sexism is not acceptable in any field. Medicine has been overtly sexist in the past. I am happy to say that in the past 15 years, women have entered medicine in greater numbers and, not surprisingly, demonstrated their capabilities. Both women and men have found it easier to enter heretofore male or female-dominated roles.

However, medicine and medical humor remain sexist to some degree. Sexism in *Medicalese* is intended to be humorous, not serious. Again, let us laugh at our quirks yet deal with our colleagues and patients in a professional and unbiased manner.

Acknowledgments

I am especially indebted to my wife, Cathy, for her professional and personal support. She is a wise and practical editor and designer of books. Cathy possesses a clear understanding of the overall process of book crafting, along with keen attention to detail.

Several individuals were kind enough to review *Medicalese* and enhance the final product with their suggestions. Reviewers include: David and Sarah James, Karen and Terry Linehan, Berry McConnell, Cecilia Graves, Jim Pierce, and Mike and Carol Marsh.

Susan Headrick was most helpful as a professional proofreader. Michael Byrd of Wordwright Publishing provided essential assistance in producing the cover for *Medicalese*.

The concept of Goosing Treatment was originally described in an article by Stuart A. Copans, entitled "Therapeutic Effects of Forceful Goosing on Major Affective Illness."

A

Aaaah......1) What the doctor tells the patient to say before gagging the patient to the max. 2) Word preceding expletive when one receives the medical bill.

Abase......The goal of the attending physician on rounds, that is to shame or embarrass low-life medical students and interns as much as possible.

Acquired Anencephaly......Anencephaly means "without a brain." Acquired anencephaly means a person is acting as if he/she is brainless. This condition is often found in hospital administrators.

Admitting Receptionist......Personnel trained to smile pleasantly while extracting promissory notes, future inheritances, gold fillings, etc., from patients prior to allowing them admission to the hospital. In the Emergency Department, admitting receptionists make sure that multiple redundant forms full of obscure and irrelevant information are filled out in triplicate before treatment is begun.

Agog......The condition of medical students during their first days in the hospital, marked by eager curiosity and extreme apprehension. In this state, students are rarely able to find bathrooms by themselves, and, if they do, they frequently enter the wrong one.

RESTROOMS

Medical students in an AGOG state search urgently for the restroom.

AMA (American Medical Association)......Powerful union responsible for keeping medicine a lucrative monopoly. AMA-sponsored research has led to the development of modern toys such as skateboards, rollerblades, hangliders, and four-wheelers, all of which help ensure a steady supply of patients.

Anesthesia......Advanced techniques used to induce numbness or an unconscious state in patients, thereby making painful procedures easier. Common anesthetic methods include: 1) Bite the Bullet, 2) Sodium None-at-All, 3) Brutane, 4) Whiskey, 5) Whang him on the head with a rubber mallet.

Anesthesiologist......Gas passer. Generally, anesthesiologists serve the same function as old time "B" movies, namely putting you to sleep. The difference in this sleep, however, is that you wake up feeling like a truck ran over you and you receive a large bill (*see* Wallet Biopsy).

Appointment......Time you are scheduled to show up in the doctor's office to begin a two-hour wait to see the doctor.

Attending Physician......The big Kahuna (medicine man), the bigwig physician who supervises the residents, interns, and medical students. Expects to be addressed as Doctor Sir, Sahib, or Bwana.

B

Babbling......Noise emanating from medical students when they are asked a question on rounds.

Barium Enema......Procedure whereby doctor attempts to make a concrete impression of the large intestine, hopefully removable. Preparation involves giving five or more laxatives the night before, so the patient is up all night running to the bathroom. The patient is then too sleepy to complain about a cold, chalky liquid being pumped in the wrong end through a tube.

Beaming Up......Not the same thing as in *Star Trek*. If a patient is "beamed up," he/she is hopefully heading upward, to the Big Hospital in the Sky. The only advantage of beaming up is that a beamed patient is no longer responsible for the hospital and doctor bills.

Bill......Paperwork mishmash mailed to patients after they are discharged from the hospital, listing every Q-tip, Band-aid, tongue blade, and dose of aspirin used during treatment. Hospitals use the **RICH** billing method: **R**edundant, **I**ncomprehensible, **C**onfusing, and **H**airsplitting. Patients are never quite sure what they are being billed for or when the billing process is complete.

Bedpan......Metal pan kept in the refrigerator, designed to keep patients from asking for assistance in going to the bathroom.

Beeper/Pager...Portable electronic signaling device used to send messages to doctors. Information sent by beeper includes stock tips, boat prices, warnings when a patient's family has arrived, etc. Occasionally, medical messages are transmitted by beeper, but these are promptly ignored and forgotten by physicians.

Doctor receiving an important message by beeper.

Doctor receiving a message of little consequence.

Black Bag......Used by doctors to carry essential items such as spare change, bagels, bottles of wine, theater tickets, and a change of underwear.

Blood......Vital life-giving substance, extracted from hospitalized patients in small quantities until it is gone.

Bonbon......Essential staple to consume while watching doctor soap operas.

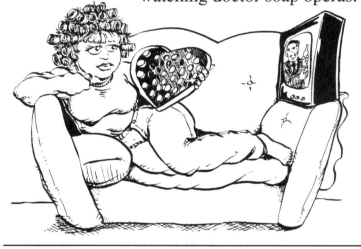

BWS (Beached Whale Syndrome)......Extremely obese patient, over 400 pounds.

B-OD (Biscuit Overdose)......Repeated overdoses on biscuits lead to the BWS.

Bulemia......Another condition often leading to the BWS, in which extremely large amounts of food are ingested at one time (such as the contents of a whole refrigerator).

C

Cafeteria......Area in which bland, tasteless, and repulsive hospital diets are designed, tested and perfected. Mean-Meow Cat Food and Goopy-Poopy Puppy Chow were discovered in hospital cafeteria food testing.

Hospital cafeteria chef carefully prepares patients' food.

CAT Scan......Fancy X-ray machine named in honor of kitty-cats sacrificed in perfecting this machine. The machine is designed to further line the pockets of radiologists, enabling them to buy antique cars, tennis courts, emeralds, etc. Computers aid the X-ray machine to make detailed pictures of the head and brain, producing exotic technical diagnoses such as airhead / peabrain / aeronaut /mush factory up top/ out to lunch permanently / light's on but nobody is home / playing without a full deck / one brick short of a full load, etc.

Capuchin......1) Small monkey trained to perform tricks on command. Paid peanuts. Same as 2) Intern.

Casteism......Use of a caste system. Originally found in India, this system has been adopted by medicine in the United States. In order of hierarchy, from top to bottom:

    (1) Attending physician = Supreme Being

    (2) Resident

    (3) Nurse

    (4) Intern

    (5) Ward clerk

    (6) Orderly

    (7) Janitor

    (8) Garbage man

    (9) Medical student = Untouchable

(In other words, a medical student is on the part of the totem pole that is buried in the ground.)

Cerumen Cerebrum......Waxhead.

Chart......Article originally designed to store information on patients, now more commonly used to hold essential hospital items such as pizza discount coupons, bookie sheets, crossword puzzles, Fig Newtons, romance novels, etc. Occasionally, patient information is still included in the chart: Essential data, such as vital signs, is often lacking and is replaced by irrelevant facts, such as how often a patient burped in the past 24 hours.

Chiropractors......Doctors specializing in bi-weekly spinal manipulations. The purpose of the manipulations is to realign the spine, and, at the same time, lighten the wallet.

Circumcision......Gruesome rite practiced by primitive tribes to initiate male infant members into the clan. The rite is performed by the tribal medicine man (doctor), who dresses in special attire (mask, gown, gloves, booties) for the ceremony. A newborn infant is strapped to a table. The medicine man applies a special paint (betadine) to the infant to ward off evil spirits (germs). The crude and primitive rite, consisting of mutilation of the infant's sexual organs, is done without anesthesia.

CME (Continuing Medical Education)......Courses doctors must attend to stay current on the latest medical treatments. Usually consists of flying to an exotic, picturesque vacation spot, followed by laying in the sun, partying until the wee hours of the morning, and visiting with old medical school buddies. There is sometimes an actual attempt to attend brief lectures on some obscure medical topic so that the whole trip may be written off on taxes.

Doctor at CME meeting, working diligently to keep up with the latest medical advances.

Codes......Signify a sudden demand for action:
- **Code Green**......Doctors head for the first hole at the country club!
- **Code Red**......Irate family member is in a patient's room!
- **Code Yellow**.....Patient may secrete bodily fluids (i.e. spit, vomit, urine) on anyone close by.
- **Code 15-91**......Good-looking nurse. I'd like to check that out!

Committee......Life form with 12 or more legs and no brains; its main function: to waste time in meetings.

Consultant......Doctor who advises the main doctor caring for a patient. The consultant is called in at the last minute to help share the blame when a patient is going bad.

Coronary Care Unit (CCU)......Heartache Hotel.

CPR (Cardiopulmonary Resuscitation)......Really stands for "Cracking Patient's Ribs," when the chest and ribs are repeatedly squashed in an attempt to wake a patient up.

Crock......A patient who continually complains of multiple symptoms which are imaginary in origin. Usually answers, "Yes!" to such questions as, "Do your teeth feel hairy?" or "Do you feel like your ankles are on upside down?" or "Do your toenails sometimes groan at night?" (*To determine if a patient is a crock, see* PORCELAIN LEVEL *and* PORCELAIN RATING SCALE.)

Compensation Neurosis......"Injury" sustained after an accident. Treated by a lawyer, not a doctor, the symptoms are relieved only when the patient receives a large greenback poultice (*see* GREENBACK POULTICE).

Compensation neurosis: **Before** *treatment with a greenback poultice.*

*Compensation neurosis: **After** treatment with a
greenback poultice.*

D

Deductible......Portion of the bill not covered by insurance. Equal to a patient's annual income or life savings, whichever is greater.

Dietitian......Person responsible for making sure that food reaching patients is without salt / sugar / fat / carbohydrates / calories, and is cold / soggy / unpalatable / tasteless. Dietitians strive to ensure that hospital food has the consistency and taste of Play-Doh.

Discharge......Event which occurs when the pocketbook or wallet is empty (*see* WALLET BIOPSY) and when patients look like drug addicts or victims of porcupine attacks (from needle sticks).

Doc-in-the-Box......Urgent care center. Also known as McDoc's, Mediquack, and Shoebox Doc Shop.

Doctor......Highly-trained professional bound by the Hippocratic Oath to practice only for the good of his/her patients. Unfortunately, doctors are paid more the sicker their patients are, rather than getting paid to keep them healthy.

Diagnosis......Label used to describe a patient's medical condition. Sometimes determined by deductive reasoning. More often, it is obtained by systems such as: 1) Throwing darts at a chart on the wall, 2) Spinning a roulette wheel, or 3) Making up the diagnosis. All three methods are sometimes utilized to give a patient multiple diagnoses, thereby maximizing payments from insurance companies.

Obtaining the diagnosis.

Doctors' Lounge......Area physicians use to escape when patients' families arrive. Doctors use the lounge to play cards, smoke cigars, tell lawyer jokes, discuss investments, and watch *General Hospital*.

Busy physicians hard at work in the Doctors' Lounge.

*Because deep down, they're really good guys.

‡Professional courtesy

◊ Only 1 in 1,000,000 do any good.

Doc-'til-you-Drop......Barbaric system used to train new doctors, whereby they work all hours of the day and night with little or no sleep. Strangely enough, doctors-in-training do not fall under public protection laws which limit the number of hours worked by airline pilots, train engineers, nuclear techs, etc.

Dodoism......A typical statement spoken by a medical student on rounds (*See* BABBLING). Examples include 1) "Maybe he's pregnant?" 2) "Ga-ga-ga-ga?" 3) "What, me worry?"

Dose......The amount of medicine it takes to quiet a patient.

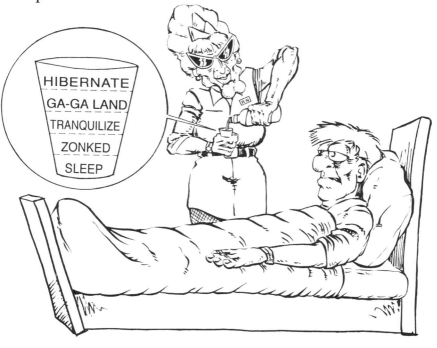

Dosing the patient adequately is a fine art.

E

EKG (Electrocardiogram).........1) Ticker tape. 2) A strip of paper with weird scrawled lines, which doctors can look at mysteriously and mumble, "Hmm, interesting. We need further tests!" while actually planning vacations, tennis dates, land purchases, etc.

Encephaloatrophy......Atrophy (wasting) of the brain substance, most often caused by watching more than two hours of TV per day.

EMG (Electromyogram)......A test of muscles and nerves involving electrical stimulation through needles. The test was invented by the Huns, who combined methods used by voodoo queens on dolls and high school anatomy students on frogs.

ER (Emergency Room)......A place you tell police you are going when you are stopped for speeding. At least two hours of sitting and waiting is usually required prior to being treated in the ER, regardless of the seriousness of the injury. Emergency Room personnel also believe that you must feel pain or you will doubt that adequate treatment has been given: Expect to have two to twelve needles stuck in various parts of your body prior to leaving the ER.

Elevator......Method of hospital travel used to irritate patients' family and friends and keep them from visiting — designed to travel very slowly to desired floors and break down between floors when full.

The hospital elevator.

Egomegaly....Personality disorder common among surgeons, involving extreme self-appreciation (massive ego).

E.T. Tube......Endotracheal or End-to-Talking tube, inserted into the trachea (windpipe) to quiet loud and complaining patients.

Excise....1) To cut out. 2) The surgeon's approach to any disease.

Enema......Device used to "treat" any patient complaining about hospital food or nursing care. Enemas work by expunging evil spirits and harmful vapors from the body (replacing leeches used for the same function years ago). Orders for enemas are generally written in code. Examples include, "Enema, 3H until 3B," which means, "Give a High, Hot, and Heavy Enema until the patient is Big, Bloated, and Bug-Eyed," or "Enema, FF/FFF," which means, "Fast and Furious Enema until the patient is Full, Floating, and Fragrant."

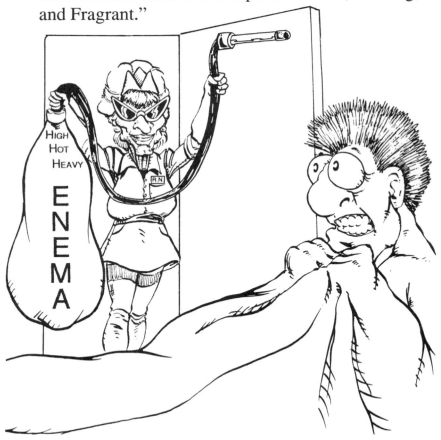

The nurse arrives with a "3H special" for the patient.

Eternal Care Unit......The only treatment area above and beyond the Intensive Care Unit. Where patients end up after the "beaming up" process.

F

Flatus......1) Vapor mixture of five gases (nitrogen, carbon dioxide, hydrogen, oxygen, and methane) found in the large intestine. 2) "Tail wind" used by joggers to increase running speed. 3) Fart.

Flatologist......Specialist in flatus. Flatology originated with the great "Father of Medicine" Hippocrates, a Greek physician who lived about 400 B.C. Hippocrates advocated medical practice based on science instead of superstition. Hippocrates wrote the famous "Hippocratic Oath," an ethical guide to young physicians about to enter the practice of medicine. The eminent Hippocrates also penned a lesser-known treatise, "The Winds," describing illnesses that result from too much gas.

FLK......Sophisticated medical terminology used to describe children whose appearance is a little out-of-the-ordinary. Stands for "Funny Looking Kid."

Floccinaucinihilipilification......The act of estimating as worthless, which is the main function performed by attending physicians on medical students.
(note: floccinaucinihilipilification is a __real__ word!)

Formication......Get your mind out of the gutter! It's not dirty. Formication is the sensation of ants crawling all over your body.

Caught in the act of formication.

Foley Catheter......Torture device held in reserve for the most difficult patients. A rubber tube is inserted into the bladder; the more unruly the patient, the larger the size of catheter used. Once in place, the tube produces the feeling of constantly having to urinate.

Fom-pee......Chinese word for flatus (fart).

Frostbite......Injury sustained from being bitten while trying to put the make on a frigid woman.

G

Gofer......Another name for medical student, as they are constantly being told to "go fer" this and "go fer" that.

G.O.K. ......Sophisticated diagnosis made on extremely difficult cases. Stands for "God Only Knows!"

Gomer.....The term GOMER originally stood for any patient you wanted to "Get Out of My Emergency Room." The label gomer has now been expanded to include patients in the hospital who are combative, abusive, irritating, agitated, and senile. (*To determine if a patient is a Gomer, see* GOMER POINT SCALE, *p. 32.*)

Gomer Point Scale......Used to determine whether a patient is truly a GOMER. A score of 8 is suggestive, 12 is definite. Examples of GOMER points include:

- Admitting orders include, "STAT BATH!".................5
- Admitting orders include, "STAT BATH, DUST FOR LICE!"......................................7
- Patient transferred to hospital after eviction from a nursing home due to poor behavior......4
- Transfer note from referring hospital ends, "sorry"...5
- Pulls out foley (urinary) catheter.........................5
- Pulls out foley with balloon still inflated...............9
- Tuberculosis discovered 1 week after successful mouth-to-mouth resuscitation.........................6
- Tuberculosis discovered 1 week after unsuccessful mouth-to-mouth resuscitation.........................9
- Spits on medical student...................................1
- Spits on nurse...4
- Spits on attending doctor.................................8
- Out of full restraints less than 5 minutes after put on...3
- Found in bed with another patient.........................6
- Bites bulb off thermometer................................3
- Bites bulb off rectal thermometer.........................5
- Has alcohol-induced flashbacks............................4
- Tells same war story three consecutive days on rounds...3
- Head or body lice acquired in the hospital...............1
- Pubic lice acquired in the hospital.......................5
- Psychiatrist refuses to see patient again after initial interview.....................................8
- EEG is flat, family says patient is better...............12

Goosing Treatment......Modern therapy used to treat depressed patients, replacing anti-depressant medication and electric shock treatments used in the past. Depressed patients are given surprise "goosing" of their derrière region five times a day. The sudden, unexpected goosing startles patients; a state of relaxation and contentment ensues, allowing patients to forget their troubles and live happily-ever-after.

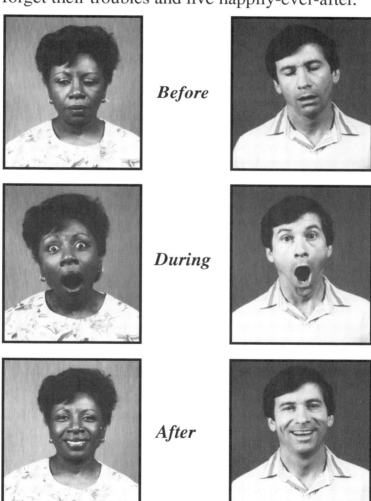

Before

During

After

Patients undergoing Goosing Treatment.

Greenback Poultice......Only definite cure for compensation neurosis (*see* COMPENSATION NEUROSIS). An "injured" person receives a large application of greenstuff (money) for treatment of "injuries" sustained in an accident. The resulting recovery is often instantaneous and miraculous.

Gynecologist......Doctor with a license to practice legalized groping and voyeurism. Prerequisite to become a gynecologist is a Peeping Tom Apprenticeship.

H

Haldol......Major tranquilizer given to unruly patients, or to doctors after they have seen 50 to 60 patients in the office in one day.

Head Nurse......Commonly known as an ogress (female of ogre). Responsibilities include snooping into the business and personal lives of patients, doctors, other nurses, and everyone else in the hospital.

Heel......Degree to which the doctor's boat is leaning to one side while sailing.

Hunky......Unskilled laborer. Same as intern.

Hospital......1) A place people actually pay big bucks to be poked, prodded, needled, interrogated, and fed miserable food, all when they are feeling their worst. 2) Overnight accommodations charging four-star-hotel prices for flea-bag facilities. 3) Institution providing supportive treatment and intensive care for doctors' and hospital administrators' bank accounts.

Hospital Administrator......Life form which views itself as superior to all other hospital personnel. In reality, hospital administrators rank equal to lice, cockroaches, and rats.

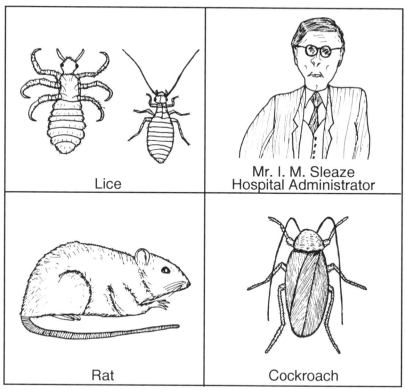

Lice

Mr. I. M. Sleaze
Hospital Administrator

Rat

Cockroach

Vermin

Housekeeping......Personnel in this department are consulted for the latest hospital gossip. They know more about the patients' problems than the doctors. Housekeeping personnel function as holder-uppers of hospital walls and keep hospital mops and brooms from moving anyplace.

Housekeeping personnel hard at "work."

I

ICU (Intensive Care Unit)......Patients are sent to the ICU when the doctor is really stuck as to what is going on (ICU = I Can't Understand). Visiting hours are severely limited so patients' families can't ask embarrassing questions or see Witch Doctor dances performed. Really sick patients are surrounded by a NASA-like array of machines, plastic tubes, and electronic gadgets so nobody can get close enough to catch what they have.

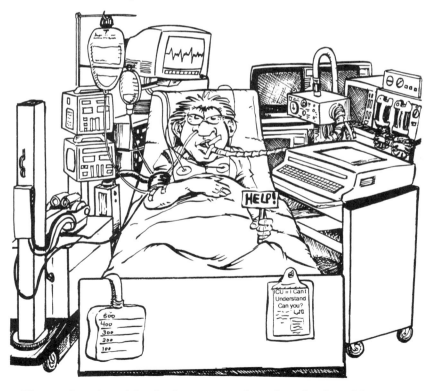

The patient is critical, since more than four body orifices are plugged by plastic tubes.

Illegible......Final goal of doctors' writing methods. Doctors spend years learning to scrawl and scribble using the CHUMP method:

C = Confusing
H = Hazy
U = Unclear
M = Muddled
P = Piccasoed

Inpatient......Where the sponge is left when the surgeon messes up.

Insipid......Adjective describing typical medical lecture — dull and uninteresting.

Intercom......Voice-box in the wall, enabling nurses, without getting up from their romance novels and bonbons, to keep patients awake at night.

Interns......First-year postgraduate doctors who are actually indentured servants (slave laborers), working for less than minimum wage. Before you let one near you, remember that he/she probably last slept three nights ago, and he/she will likely poke and probe EVERY part and orifice of the body. Interns are often heard singing "I'm a Scut Monkey" to the tune of "I'm a Girl Watcher." Other names for intern are: scutpuppy, lackey, grumphie, footboy, bohunk, capuchin, losel, and low-life.

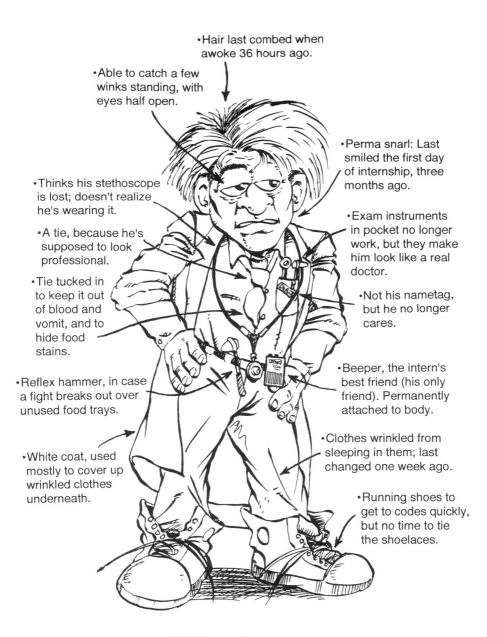

Modern-Day Intern

Intern Teaching Award......This prestigious award is given annually to the one person who contributes most to the education of the interns during their training. Most often, it goes to a local drunk, who has had twenty-seven admissions for pancreatitis and alcohol withdrawal during the past year.

IOFB......Post-vasectomy patient. Stands for "I Only Fire Blanks," and means you never have to say you're sorry.

Ipecac-Wire Treatment......This form of "therapy" was devised by brilliant medical students at Ohio State University in 1977, to repay a particularly nasty attending physician. First, a person's jaw is wired shut. Ipecac, to induce vomiting, is then given unknowingly to the person in a drink taken through a straw.

IPPB......Treatment given by respiratory therapist: Air and medication are forced under pressure into the lungs. Stands for "I Prevent Possible Breathing."

IV (Intravenous) Equipment......IV fluids are used to flush bad humors from the body and sustain patients in the likely event that they are unable to keep down hospital food. IV needles are scientifically designed to jump out of the vein within one hour of insertion, enabling medical students to practice IV sticks and nurses to punish unruly patients.

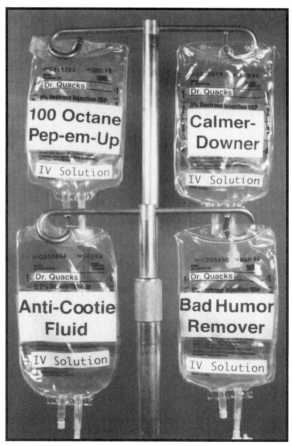

Common IV fluids

J

Jive......Type of talk used by interns and residents on nurses, in attempts to lure them back to the couch in pathology.

Jactitation......Repetitive movements, near-convulsive in nature, often seen emanating from the pathology couch when jive is successful.

Jargon......Obscure and often pretentious language, used frequently in medical discussions; also known as medicalese. For example, to describe a "pimple on the big toe," a doctor would say, "a pustular papule on the medial appendage of the distal extension off the lower extremity." Or, to say, "The patient's treatment didn't work," a doctor would drone, "The patient responded suboptimally to our therapeutic regimen."

Jackals' Law......All bleeding stops sooner or later.

Jugulate......To suppress disease by extreme measures — a common practice in medicine today. The extraordinary treatments are, unfortunately, oftentimes worse than the diseases themselves.

K

Kids' Rebound Law......No matter how sick a child looks at home, by the time the child is brought to the Emergency Room and examined by the doctor, the child appears completely healthy.

Kuru......Rapidly progressive disease of the brain, nearly always fatal, transmitted by cannibalism. Symptoms include a lack of sense, gnawing hunger, and love of fellow man.

L

Laparotomy......The "I don't know what's going on, but maybe if we cut in here, we'll find something" operation.

Law of Fives......If five or more plastic tubes are inserted into body orifices, the situation is critical.

Lead Poisoning......Disorder characterized by abdominal pain and impairment of the nervous system, most often seen in adults playing with guns (as in lead bullets).

Labor......Term used to make the birth process seem like a simple act of work. In reality, LABOR stands for **L**ong **A**nd **B**rutal **O**rdeal for **R**eal. Synonyms include: Awful Agony, Piercing Pain, and Terrible Torture.

Ob-Gyn Doctors use technical terms to describe three stages of labor. The three stages are better understood in terms of what they feel like to the mother. Stage One: "Severe cramps becoming longer and more frequent." Stage Two: "Awful, continuous pain and pressure, like all your insides are getting ready to burst." Stage Three: "Like a cinder block is coming out your bottom end."

Lalorrhea......Excessive flow of words, often without meaning (as in BS). Common verbal practice of hospital administrators.

Liniment......Medicinal liquid sold as a "cure-all" in the old days. Replaced by modern and more expensive entities such as Geritol and Ben-Gay. The modern entities are thought to be almost as effective as the old-time elixirs.

Liquid Diet......"Special" diet given to patients to make sure they do not wish to stay in the hospital too long, and to make sure they are happy when they do get to go home and eat some decent food.

L.P.N.......Nursing certificate obtained after one-year understudy in Albanian Dungeons. Stands for Low-Paid Nurse or Lower Peon Nurse.

Leeching......Until the 19th century, this method of treating diseases used leeches to drain blood from the body. Leeching has since been replaced by more modern treatments, such as electroconvulsive therapy (shock treatments), onychectomy (removal of finger and toenails), and craniotomy (placement of burr holes in the head).

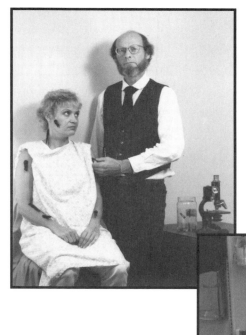

Leeching
(old-time treatment)

Burr Holes
(modern-day treatment)

M

Mammogram......Special torture device designed by chauvinist research doctors, used exclusively on women. Women are first trained from childhood to protect their breasts, to never let them be squeezed hard or bruised. Ladies are then subjected to the psychological and physical cruelty of mammography: Their breasts are compressed between two hard plates until their bosoms are swollen and discolored. The test is deemed successful if the female patient screams in agony, cries "Uncle," or passes out cold.

M.D. ....Medical Degree obtained through long years of study or for $7.98 with a mail-in coupon off a matchbook cover. Also stands for Mad Dog / Mostly Dumb / Money Digger / Mildly Demented.

MRI......Stands for **M**aximize **R**adiologists' Income. Sophisticated test using magnetic fields to make pictures of patients' insides. Operates along the same lines as an Etch-a-Sketch toy.

Medical Insurance......Payment plan designed to cover all illnesses except the one which causes you to be admitted to the hospital.

Medical Excuses......Exotic diseases you can tell your employer or school you are afflicted with in order to get time off.

- Scarabiasis = Condition in which the intestine is invaded by the dung beetle.
- Schistosomiasis = Parasitic disease due to infestation of blood flukes (snails).
- Tularemia = Infection, accompanied by high fever, caught while skinning dead rabbits.

Medical Insults......Medical terms used by doctors and nurses as insults. The terms are used for hospital administrators, ex-spouses, and patients, without the recipients being aware the terms are derogatory.

- dolor rectalis = pain in the rear end
- supratentorially deficient = lack of brains
- encephalon eccentric = weird
- schistoglossia = split (forked) tongue; not truthful
- premature senescence = early senility
- somasthenic = chronic body weakness
- sphincter algie = pain in the a_ _
- rectal-cranial inversion = head up the a_ _
- tabid = affected with syphilis
- endriloides parvus = looks like a penis, only smaller
- eupraxia deficient = incoordinated
- leptocortex = small-brained
- lipomatoid = fat
- non compos mentis = not possessed of sound mind
- pachycephalic = thick-skulled
- pneumocrania = airhead

Medical Insurance Companies......Organizations employing people who specialize in reviewing bills sent for payment. Areas of specialization include: 1) Devising confusing forms, 2) Losing copies of bills, 3) Delaying payment, 4) Referring complaints to another department, 5) Rejecting payment on the basis of obscure clauses in fine print.

Medical Phrases......Key phrases, with hidden meaning, spoken by hospital personnel.

- "We need to draw a little blood." = The blood bank is low. We're taking a gallon.
- "This may hurt just a little bit." = Get a bullet to bite on; this will feel like somebody dropped a piano on your big toe.
- "Need to run some more tests." = I don't know what's going on, but if I stall long enough, the patient is bound to get better on his own.
- "You need to stay in the hospital a while longer." = The payments on my new Mercedes are outrageous. Somebody has to pay.
- "This shot can't go in your arm." = Drop your drawers, show me your moon, and get ready to be launched off the bed.
- "The doctor is still tied up." = The doctor hasn't finished the back nine yet.
- "It's a virus." = I have no idea what's causing your symptoms, so I'll blame it on a virus.
- "The baby looks just like his father." = What an ugly baby: no hair, no teeth, and a pot belly.

Medical Records......Area in which important details of patients' records are stored and often put through 3M processing (Mutilated, Misplaced, and Misfiled).

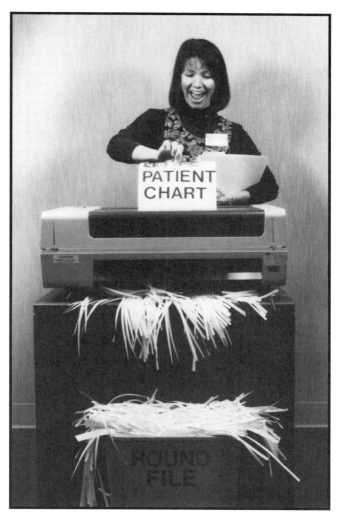

*Medical Records personnel provide special
3M care for patients' records.*

Medical School......Instruction that is similar to fraternity hazing, except it lasts four years.

Medical Students......Highly irritating, sub-human life forms, constantly in a daze, often seen running into a bathroom (often the wrong one) with anxious bowels. Also known as scumworms, scrofulous dogs, or smurfballs, medical students must be stupid enough to pay large amounts of money to be put through long hours of work and abuse. Medical students are easy to spot on medical rounds, where, due to extreme anxiety, they babble incessantly and irrelevantly when asked questions. Other synonyms include nidget, gofer, pissant, prattler, puler, schmo, and mutant.

Medicalese......Medical gibberish talk, which mainly consists of using more and bigger words in place of fewer and smaller words in order to sound mysterious and impressive. An example would be: "As I was examining the patient's upper extremity, noting the erythematous adiaphoretic appearance of the integument, accompanied by contusions, her mandible separated from her maxilla and her mouth opened involuntarily." This is the same as: "As I looked at her arm, seeing red, dry skin and bruises, she yawned."

Doctors also use medicalese to maximize reimbursement. Simple illnesses are described in technical medical terms: A cold becomes a "viral upper respiratory infection," and a bad sore throat becomes "severe infectious pharyngitis."

Midwife......Doctor's second wife, coming after the first wife (who was dumped after putting the doctor through long years of schooling), and before the last wife (the young pretty thing the doctor marries in his declining, senile years).

Morning Sickness......Term coined by male Ob-gyn doctors who have never experienced this affliction, which is rarely limited to morning nausea. The medical term for morning sickness, Hyperemesis Gravidarum (meaning *multiple* and *repeated* bouts of vomiting during pregnancy), provides a somewhat more accurate description. The new lay term, "Three-to-Six Month, 24-Hour-a-Day Upchuck Syndrome," paints an even clearer picture of this malady.

Mooitis......Uncontrollable urge to moo whenever cows are observed.

Moo ooooooooooooooo......

Morgue......Part of the hospital that certain people just seem to be dying to get in. Some people will go to any lengths to escape paying their bills.

N

Night Supervisor......Person responsible for making sure night nurses are staying awake and doing their job, namely, keeping patients awake.

Nicknames......Most medical specialists have shorter or more sensible names:
- anesthesiologist = gas passer
- dentist = tooth carpenter
- dermatologist = zitman
- internist = flea
- neurologist = neuron
- orthopedist = jock-doc or sawbones
- psychiatrist = shrink
- radiologist = raydoc
- surgeon = blade or hack
- urologist = peetotaler

No-Code......If a patient is designated a "no-code," then aggressive life support procedures are withheld. Simple tests are used to determine a patient's code status, including, 1) Can the patient identify pictures of Mickey Mouse, Goofy and Donald Duck? 2) Does the patient know what is better than sailing, golf, and tennis? If the patient doesn't know Disney characters and sex, there is no reason to use aggressive therapy, and the patient is made a "no-code."

No-No Phrases......Medical students are taught from Day One <u>not</u> to say certain words or remarks. The Top Ten No-No Phrases that you never hear a doctor utter in the hospital are:

1) Uh-oh!
2) Oops!
3) There seems to be an awful lot of bleeding here!
4) Guess we made a mistake.
5) I don't know.
6) This will hurt a lot.
7) This will hurt you more than it will hurt me.
8) What do we do now?
9) Look at my hands shake.
10) I think it's too late.

Professor-Dr. G. instructs medical students
on "No-No" phrases.

Nurse......1) Expert trained to be bossy and to punish patients with shots, IVs, enemas, cattle prods, horse whips, etc. The best nurses are large, gruff, tuff, and able to lift a baby grand piano with a single hand. 2) Person capable of healing sick people despite the direct supervision of a physician.

Student Nurse *in training, typically a sweet, innocent young thing who is rapidly trained to be a.....*

***Real Nurse**, a sour, bossy, mean old thing.*

Nurse Call-Button......Small signaling device strategically placed just out of a patient's reach. Even when located and pressed, the button turns on a light in the nursing station, which nurses are trained to ignore.

O

Omphaloskepsis......Home treatment method which originated in the mysterious Far East and subsequently spread rapidly to the Modern West. Omphaloskepsis, which can be practiced at home or at work, consists of the contemplation of one's navel as part of a mystical exercise.

On-Call......An "on-call" doctor accepts urgent calls from patients during night and weekend hours. This means that if you call Dr. OnCall about little Johnny waking up in the middle of the night with a high fever, rest assured that you will receive a call back by the time A) Johnny has his next birthday, or B) Johnny is completely well.

Obstetricians......Baby-catcher specialists, experts in wrenching neonates out of mothers. Evolved from lobster technicians, experts in wrenching lobsters out of lobster pots.

Olfactometer......Device used by doctors to determine the truthfulness of Old Wives' Tales and medical journal articles.

Ophthalmologist......Wouldn't it be easier to say and spell eye doctor? The term was invented by eye doctors to provide themselves with an air of importance and mystique. The word also minimizes complaints about their astronomical fees because not too many people can say ophthalmologist, much less spell it.

Ophthalmoscope......Instrument used to look inside a patient's eyes, to see if "the light is on but nobody is home" or "playing a good second base, but it's football season."

*Doctor using an **ophthalmoscope** to examine a patient.*

O.R. Tech......Operating room technicians are paid to absorb the wrath and anger of the "High and Mighty Surgeon" in the operating room. They can be identified by the absence of certain body parts (ears, fingers, hands, etc.), cut off by surgeons in fits of rage, and by the presence of a perma-grin smile (being forced to listen to barrages of lousy jokes told by surgeons).

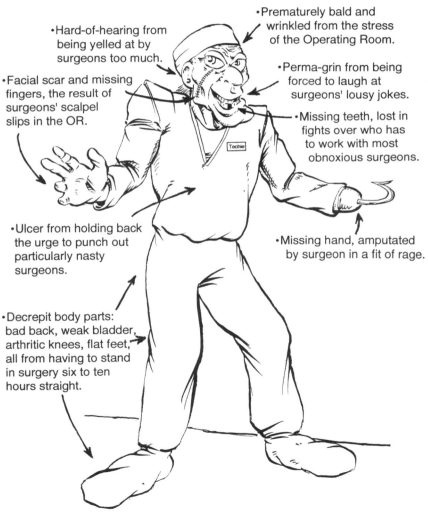

•Hard-of-hearing from being yelled at by surgeons too much.

•Prematurely bald and wrinkled from the stress of the Operating Room.

•Facial scar and missing fingers, the result of surgeons' scalpel slips in the OR.

•Perma-grin from being forced to laugh at surgeons' lousy jokes.

•Missing teeth, lost in fights over who has to work with most obnoxious surgeons.

•Ulcer from holding back the urge to punch out particularly nasty surgeons.

•Missing hand, amputated by surgeon in a fit of rage.

•Decrepit body parts: bad back, weak bladder, arthritic knees, flat feet, all from having to stand in surgery six to ten hours straight.

Ophthalmolock......Locking of the eyes onto an attractive body part on a person of the opposite sex.

Outpatient......What the hospital administrator would like to tell patients who can't pay their bills.

O2......Oxygen. Given by mask or nasal prongs, oxygen is thought to enable patients to breathe better by dissolving boogers.

Ouch Words......Words or phrases which cause a physician to cringe. If too many of these words are spoken in one utterance, total breakdown of a physician can result. The Top Ten Ouch Words are:

- litigation
- lawsuit
- malpractice
- audit
- IRS
- "missing a sponge"
- "operated on the wrong leg"
- "she has no insurance"
- taxes
- alimony

Ornithologist......Bird watcher. Not a doctor (of medicine) at all, dummy. If your doctor's diploma says ornithologist, find a new doctor, quick!

Osteopath......Doctor believing in the human body's power to heal itself, thereby overcoming injuries and infections. Osteopathic theory has clearly been proven incorrect by the miracle of modern TV: Television commercials document that the answer to life's problems is either A) Take a pill, or B) Buy some expensive and unneeded item for yourself.

Otolaryngologist......What a mouthful. Not much better saying, "Ear, Nose, and Throat Doctor," but what can one expect from doctors who spend their time messing around in people's throats and noses?

Otoscope......Instrument jammed into the ear to examine the ear drum, pack down ear wax, and to check whether a patient has peas, marbles, cobwebs, brains, or nothing between the ears.

*Doctor using an **otoscope** to examine a patient.*

Otoselecta......Ear selection, a common condition in children ages 3 through 30. The ears of affected individuals elect to hear what they like and ignore the rest.

Otomassage......Ear massage. Telling people what they want to hear.

Ozonometer......Instrument used by psychiatrists to determine how far out in the ozone a patient is.

P

Paging System......Use of hospital loudspeakers to make it sound like important and official business is routinely taking place in the hospital. Some poor flunky is hired to sit in an empty room and give fictitious pages such as: "Dr. Busy, to the ER, Stat!", "Code Red — room 100!", or "Mr. Dee Ceased, call the morgue."

Pathologist......Doctors who look like they have been puttering away with formaldehyde-soaked body parts in the dark and dingy hospital basement. Pathologists look like this because *that's exactly what they have been doing!* Pathologists are stuck with this job because they often have previously flunked out of embalming school.

Panhandler......Nurses' Aide.

Patient Medicalese......Slight alterations in medical terms, spoken by patients or their families.

- "De Beetles" = diabetes
- "Vomik" = vomit
- "Smiling mighty Jesus" = spinal meningitis
- "ProstRate gland" = prostate gland
- "Sick-as-hell crisis" = sickle cell crisis
- "Chicken Pops" = chicken pox
- "High Anus Hernia" = hiatal hernia
- "An awful erection" = anaphylactic reaction
- "Massive internal fart" = myocardial infarction
- "Flea bites" = phlebitis
- "Very close veins" = varicose veins
- "Infantigo" = Impetigo
- "Emeralds" = hemorrhoids
- "Youth in Asia" = euthanasia
- "Old-timers disease" = Alzheimer's disease

Pathodixia......A preoccupation with exhibiting one's injured or diseased part.

PBTB......Expression used when the situation is hopeless, when the Beaming Up process is approaching. Stands for "Pine Box to Bedside."

Pediatrician......Masochistic physician whose duties include: 1) Being attacked by ankle-biters and knee-knockers, 2) Being constantly awakened by anxious mothers, 3) Being vomited or peed upon by little ones. The advantage pediatricians enjoy, that many of their patients can't talk and complain, is offset by hysterical parents talking enough for twenty people.

Patient......1) Guinea pig. 2) Person with responsibility of keeping doctors, nurses, and administrators employed and well-paid.

Phlebotomist......Fancy name for blood drawers, persons trained to poke needles into patients' arms until they scream for mercy or until no blood is left to remove. Many phlebotomists have prominent incisor teeth and ancestors from Transylvania.

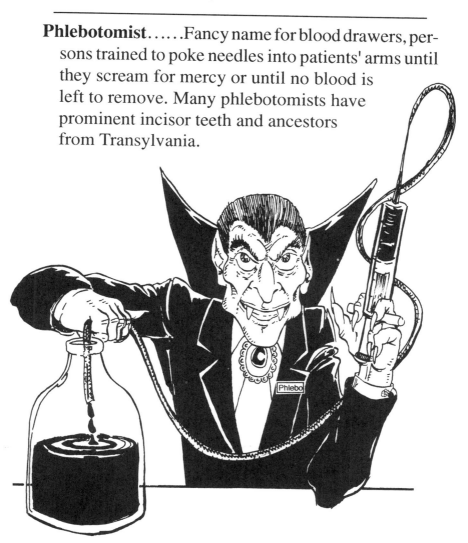

Upon withdrawal of a "small amount" of blood from the patient, a phlebotomist uses the blood to "run a few tests."

Physical Therapy......Specialized treatment area which evolved from medieval torture chambers. Patients are first put through extreme and unnatural movements, with resulting muscle stiffness, joint swelling, and bodily pain. The patient is then given massage, whirlpool baths, ultrasonic vibration treatment, etc., to make the patient forget the abuse and believe that the therapy is actually helping.

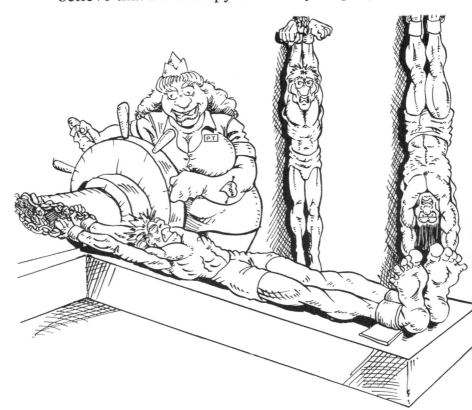

Physical terrorist applying "high-tech" stretching equipment to patients.

Pes Rictus Malady......Also known as foot-in-mouth disease. Often results from asking the wrong question such as, "How many months pregnant are you?" ("I'm not pregnant, doctor"), or "Are you the patient's father?" ("No, I'm her husband").

Pharmacist......Highly-trained professional who spent five years in college learning how to read doctors' prescriptions and count pills from a big bottle into a little bottle.

Physician......1) Egomaniac. 2) Megalomaniac. 3) Maxillomegaloegomaniac.

Pong/Pool......The primary activity of medical students on a psychiatry rotation. The ping-pong and billiards tables on the psychiatric wards are in almost continuous use by students.

Paramedic......Advanced EMT (Elderly Mobile Transportation) specialist.

Plutotosis......Breath like Pluto the Dog's.

Pneumocrania......Airhead.
Pneumocraniology......Study of airheads.

Poikilocardic......Cold-hearted.

Porcelain Level......Blood test requested by a doctor if a patient is thought to be a "crock" (*see* CROCK): The higher the porcelain level, the more "crocky" a patient is.

Patient in need of a porcelain level blood test to determine extent of crockism.

Porcelain Rating Scale......Another method of determining whether a patient is a crock. Points are assigned to various complaints that patients voice. A score of 5 strongly suggests a patient is a crock; a score of 7 is definite evidence. Examples of complaints scoring crock points are:

- "Toenails burn all night.".......................................3
- "Heart keeps beating in an SOS pattern.".............5
- "I have a thirteen-page list of problems
  here, doctor."...3
- "Oh, my head. My feet. My toes. My legs. My
  arms. My neck. My eyes. My eyelashes. My
  fingernails. Just *everything* hurts.".................4
- "I won't be happy unless you find
  something wrong with me.".............................3
- "Hair is growing too loud.".................................4
- "Severe diarrhea after taking a laxative for
  my constipation."...1
- "I've been to six doctors here in town, plus
  the Mayo Clinic and Johns Hopkins. I just
  know *you* can find out what's wrong
  with me, even if the others couldn't. ".............3
- "Keep waking up because I forget to breathe.".......4
- "Have to make myself gag down third helpings."....2
- "I don't eat a thing; it's my thyroid gland that
  causes me to gain all this weight.".................2
- "Bubbles appear when I urinate in the toilet.".......3
- "My nose hairs hurt."...4

*NOTE: All points double if the doctor is called with a
complaint after midnight.*

Pre-Med Student......Individuals competing in the game to win entrance to medical school. The winners are usually the most obsessive-compulsive and cunning or have wealthy relatives who can influence the medical school admissions committee. Other names for a pre-med student include: prodigal wimp, med-nerd, tampie, and rabid-brain.

Prescription......Mysterious scrawls and scribbles, a combination of pig Latin and hieroglyphics, which a doctor trains for years to learn how to write. A pharmacist studies for years to learn how to decipher the gibberish. Rather than use plain English, physicians and pharmacists collaborate to maintain an air of importance and power by using their own secret language.

Prescription jabberwocky.

Prognosis....The art of foretelling the probable course of a disease and how a patient will fare with that disease in the future. Doctors typically obtain a prognosis by using a Ouija board or looking into a crystal ball.

Doctor attempting to determine the **prognosis** *of a patient.*

Potion......A large dose of liquid medicine such as castor oil or cod liver oil. These potions are as effective as expensive, modern-day wonder drugs.

Practice......The exercise of the practice of medicine by established physicians. The question is, if medicine is such a science, why is it still called practice? Don't doctors get enough practice in medical school?

Primary Care....A primary care doctor is one trained in general medical care without a distinct area of specialization. The primary care of doctors, however, includes tennis, skiing, sailing, golf, etc.

Proctologist....Doctor who specializes in the rectum as a (w)hole. The question is, who would want to specialize in proctology?

Prog......To prowl about for food. Common activity among interns and residents, who may be seen raiding nursing station refrigerators, patients' food trays, and vending machines. Similar to the behavior of bears at garbage dumps.

PTF Therapy......Special type of respiratory treatment designed to handle the most unruly patients, enemies of nurses, rabid raccoons, etc. Stands for "Pillow To Face" therapy and usually quiets the victim rapidly.

Putamen......Part of the brain recently shown to regulate common sense. Studies have documented atrophy (wasting away) of the putamen in some subjects, leading to a lack of sense. In a small number of cases, the cause of the deterioration is congenital (present at birth). More often, the brain injury is caused by consuming excessive amounts of fast food.

Pyalgia......Pain in the butt. Occasionally used to describe a condition affecting the derriére, but more often used to describe a person's overall personality.

Psychiatrist......Doctor who specializes in the mental workings. As with all physicians, proficient in complicating simple terms and concepts into medicalese (medical gibberish double-talk). Psychiatrists use expressions such as manic-depressive, paranoid schizophrenia, hysterical conversion reaction, etc., when all nutty patients can actually be classified as either bonkers, wacko, or crackers.

Psychiatrist struggling to make the correct diagnosis on a patient.

Q

Q-Fever......Infectious disease acquired from close contact with infected goats, cows, or sheep. Tell your boss you have Q-Fever, and you'll have no problem getting a week off to recover in the Bahamas (but your boss may call the Humane Society).

Quack......One who pretends to have skill in medicine. Synonyms: doctor, physician.

Quarantine......Method whereby patients' spouses, children, and pets are kept as hostages until hospital bills are paid.

Quickening......1) First movements of the fetus felt during pregnancy. 2) Sudden internal feeling of doom, accompanied by a rapid pulse, experienced upon receiving the hospital bill just prior to discharge.

Quotes......There are several quotes that help one to better understand medicine:
• "The internist knows all and does nothing."
• "The surgeon knows nothing and does everything."
• "The pathologist knows everything and does everything, but too late."
• "The nurse does it all and gets none of the credit."

R

Radiologist......Doctor who prefers to deal with pictures of people rather than the people themselves.

Reflex Hammer......Simple, primitive instrument used to hit patients, especially if they complain. Doctors are trained to find specific pressure points to strike, causing uncontrolled movements, thereby showing doctors' magical power over patients.

Resident......Young doctor-in-training who devises experiments to run on patients. A resident generally possesses unlimited, irrelevant scientific information but little practical and useful knowledge of the practice of medicine. A resident is also known as a Junior Doctor or Minor MD.

Respirator......Device used to pump air in and out of patients' lungs, enhancing bill collection and quieting loud patients. Patients refusing to hand over the family jewels or life savings can be threatened with being blown up to the size of a blimp or having the plug on the respirator pulled.

Respiratory Therapist......Another torture expert, a respiratory terrorist is skilled in using needle sticks, back blows, breathing mistreatments, blow bottles, etc., to make patients eager for discharge from the hospital. Like other ancillary personnel, respiratory therapists are trained to answer, "I'll call a nurse," if asked questions such as, "Could you pour me a glass of water?" or, "Could you hand me the bedpan?"

R.N. ......Degree obtained after two to four years of studying torture methods. Stands for Real Nasty / Rarely Nice / Raw Ninny / Really Neurotic.

Rounds......A series of very brief stops that doctors make in patients' rooms. Rounds are done as rapidly as possible so as not to miss the morning tee time or tennis date.

S

Screaming Meemies......1) Patients on a psych ward. 2) Patients in pediatricians' offices. 3) Medical students during finals week.

Scopophobia......Fear of being stared at.

Scut......Everyday tasks an intern must perform. Includes such chores as wheeling patients to X-ray, filling out lab slips, writing orders for laxatives, calling for lab test results, holding retractors in surgery, mopping floors, and the like. Ninety-eight percent of the intern's time in the hospital is spent doing scut.

Sedative......Medication given to patients so nurses will have ample time to cross-stitch, work crossword puzzles, and watch soap operas. Multiple levels of sedation can be obtained, including:
- Mostly Mellow
- Real Relaxed
- Muted and Muffled
- Purely Placid
- Slumbering Serenely
- Totally Tranquilized
- Largely Lethargic
- Completely Comatose
- Hibernating like a Bear

Sigmoidoscope......Also known as the Long Silver Bullet, this instrument was adapted from an ancient Chinese torture ritual. A sigmoidoscope enables a doctor to peer into a patient's bowels from the bottom end, greatly embarrassing the patient at the same time. A sigmoidoscope is most effective if used on a patient in front of large crowds, including student nurses, enemies of the patient, housekeeping personnel, court jesters, and TV news reporters. (Onlookers are encouraged to whisper and giggle while pointing at the patient.)

*The **sigmoidoscope**, AKA the Long Silver Bullet, at ready.*

Stethoscope......Instrument used to plug doctors' ears in order to muffle patients' complaints and families' questions. Gives doctors time to think about buying new cars, setting up tee times, etc., while appearing to be listening to sounds inside patients. To get your doctor's attention, scream/moan/belch loudly while being examined with the stethoscope, as these sounds will be intensified many times normal. Also, if the doctor fails to place any part, or the correct part, of the stethoscope in his/her ears upon examination, change doctors immediately! The stethoscope is often placed in the refrigerator for half an hour prior to being used to elicit the maximum patient response.

*Doctor using a **stethoscope** to examine a patient.*

STAT....Term used by a doctor or nurse to order that a test be done immediately, at once. The ward clerk re-interprets STAT to mean **S**ome **T**ime, **A**ny **T**ime. By the time a STAT test is requested by the ward clerk, done by the lab, and put on the chart by medical records, the patient has usually been home for three days.

Staff......Large wooden stick used by nurses to prod and beat uncooperative patients.

Sleeping Pill......Medication given when the patient is awakened shortly after falling asleep at night. Designed to keep the patient groggy through morning rounds, so the doctor is asked fewer questions.

Student Nurse......Sweet, demure, innocent young thing who is rapidly trained to be a sour, bossy, mean old thing.

Suppository......Medicine that goes in the end opposite the mouth. Contrary to the practice of some persons, it does not need to be held in with the thumb until dissolved.

Surgical Waiting Room......Area designed to function as a stage for surgeons, who appear in funny-looking clothes and dramatically tell the family, "It was nip-and-tuck; only *I* could have saved her; we're not out of the woods yet." Usually, the surgical waiting room is smokier than poolrooms in bars.

Surgeons......Arrogant, boorish, loud and obnoxious doctors, who are never happy unless they are "performing" in their "theater" (doing surgery), up to their elbows in blood and guts.

After surgery, the Great and Glorious Surgeon often makes an appearance in the surgical waiting room. Here, he extolls his own virtues and leads the faithful in praises to himself.

T

Tachylawsy.....Similar to tachycardia (fast heart rate) and tachypnea (fast breathing). Tachylawsy is usually exhibited by heavyset, older ladies, who, when asked what is wrong, say, "Oh, Lawsy, Lawsy, Lawsy, Lawsy, what ain't wrong?"

Thermometer......Small glass stick used to awaken patients at night. May be placed in one of several body orifices: Always remember R is for Red is for Rectal, and don't let a sleepy nurse stick a red one in your mouth!

Tobacco Blight......1) Disease affecting tobacco plants, causing the tobacco leaves to shrivel up and turn brown. 2) Disease affecting people using tobacco products, causing their brains to shrivel up and turn brown.

Toxic Spermosis......Syndrome seen exclusively in post-adolescent males. A lack of sex results in a buildup of sperm in the body. Eventually sperm cells overflow into the brain, blocking synapses between brain cells. The blockage results in an inability to think about anything but sex.

Terminal Flatulence (TF)......The production of large amounts of flatus (intestinal gas) from ingestion of beans, onions, cabbage, greens, etc. Signs of TF include loss of friends, cracked toilet seats, dying house plants, and rapid emptying of elevators. TF is not a good diagnosis to see written on a roommate's chart when sharing a room.

Signs of Terminal Flatulence

Tongue Blade......Big popsicle stick which is jammed into a patient's throat, bringing the patient to the point of severe gagging and tears within seconds. Also used by hospital personnel in arts-and-crafts projects in their spare time.

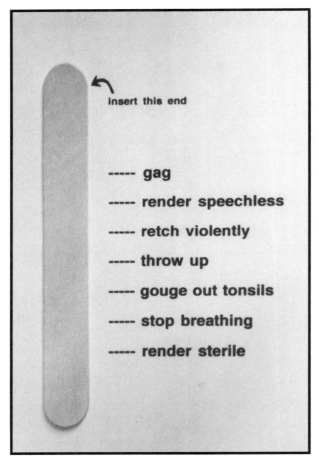

insert this end

----- **gag**

----- **render speechless**

----- **retch violently**

----- **throw up**

----- **gouge out tonsils**

----- **stop breathing**

----- **render sterile**

*A doctor inserts a **tongue blade** to achieve the desired effect on the patient.*

True Medical Excuses......Names of exotic conditions that can be given to one's employer when calling in sick at 8A.M. These excuses will scare and impress but are not total fabrication.

- Schizotrichia = Having split ends of hair: "My schizotrichia is flaring up again."
- Sternutation = Sneezing: "I had sternutations all day yesterday."
- Trypanosomiasis = Sleeping sickness: "I can't help being late for work again. I have trypanosomiasis."
- Sitomania = Periodic abnormal craving for food: "I suffered from sitomania yesterday, and I was miserable afterward."
- Ergasiophobia = Aversion to work of any kind: "My case of ergasiophobia is active again."
- Anapareunia = Lack of sex: "I was severely depressed because of my continuing anapareunia."

Treatment orifice......Body opening of any type, considered fair game for obstructing with plastic tubes by interns and residents.

Twinkie toxemia....Ingestion of excessive amounts of Twinkies and similar plastic-wrapped junk food leads to deposits of a gummy substance called trollputty in brain cells. Trollputty accumulation in areas such as the cerebral cortex, cerebellum, and humpocampus results in a loss of intelligence, balance, and sexual desire.

U

Ulysses Syndrome......Occurs when a slightly elevated lab test is discovered on a perfectly healthy person. Involves a long, expensive, and potentially dangerous workup by overeager interns and residents, without anything ever being found wrong.

Ultrasonic Undulation......The production in the infant of a primal cry of exactly 30,000 MHz energy level, which finds a receptor exclusively in the midbrain of the infant's parents.

Uncut......Condition of a patient thought to be hazardous by surgeons; surgeons usually take immediate measures to correct this situation.

Undy Alert......Occurs when a patient is seriously injured and rendered unconscious, then stripped of clothes during treatment in the Emergency Department. If the patient's underwear is dirty or torn, the patient's mother and/or fiancée are notified immediately. A notice of this serious social blunder is also placed in the patient's hometown newspaper.

Uvula......Got your mind in the gutter again, eh? The uvula is that funny little appendage hanging down from the back of your mouth. The vulva is that other one you were thinking of.

V

Vainglorious.......1) Boastfully vain and proud of oneself. 2) Arrogant. 3) Surgeon.

Vermin.......Small animals with destructive and troublesome habits. Includes cockroaches, lice, rats, and hospital administrators.

Vital Signs......Measurements a nurse checks every few hours to make sure you haven't been *beamed up* to the Final Resting Ground. If the nurse gets real sweaty, calls the doctor, and says something like, "I think he's going to bite the big cookie," after checking your vital signs, hope that you have been good enough in your lifetime to get *beamed up*, not *sent down.*

Villein....In 13th century England, villein were serf peasants who were freemen to all except their lord, to whom they remained subject as slaves. In modern times, villeins are interns, who are freemen to all except their hospital, to which they remain slaves.

Vivisection......To perform a cutting operation on a living animal for purposes of experimentation, which is the preferred method surgeons use to deal with patients who don't pay their bills.

Vulva......Look it up in a real dictionary!

W, X & Y

Wallet Biopsy......Most important procedure done in the hospital, whereby all dirty green paper and loose silver is extracted from the leather object in a patient's pocket or purse.

X-Chromosome......The little piece that makes one sassy, seductive, bewitching, demanding, and wild with a charge card.

X-ray Department......What would you expect from a place with an ominous and mysterious name like "X-ray"? This department takes patients and puts special dyes in the mouth, bottom end, and veins, then exposes the patients to radiation, producing weird images of their insides.

Yacht......1) Beloved play-toy of many physicians. Once on it, they cannot be reached. 2) Hole in the water, into which patients' money is thrown.

Y-Chromosome......The little piece that makes one an MMCP (macho male chauvinist pig).

Ward Clerk......Nursing station secretary, trained to obstruct the actual practice of medicine by requiring at least eight different forms to be filled out for any test or procedure and by tying up the nursing station phone 98% of the time. Persons with intelligence levels above that of squids are discouraged from applying for ward clerk positions; airheads and space cadets make excellent candidates.

Ward clerk hard at work , discussing the latest scandals on TV soap operas.

Z

Zippo-Brain Syndrome......Ailment common among Bosses. Caused by the ancient, barbaric, and nonsensical habit of wearing neckties. Studies show that neckties constrict arteries supplying the brain, resulting in brain-dead behavior.

Zoanthropy......Delusion that one is an animal; can be real or faked. Most often patients take on the behavior of a dog, speaking with barks and crawling about on all fours. If a patient also eats from a doggie bowl on the floor and uses a fire hydrant to do his/her business, then the delusion is very likely real.

Zoning Out......Also known as *circling the drain, Humpty-Dumptying, calling for a beam-up,* or *buying the farm*. Patients should avoid zoning out at all costs.

Tips
to improve your hospital stay:

1) Don't get sick in early July. Brand new medical students and interns begin their tour of duty on July first. Entering the hospital at this time may be hazardous to one's health.

2) Enter the hospital as a doctor instead of a patient. Doctors wear nifty white coats instead of frumpy gowns, and it's much better to cut than to be cut upon.

3) Remember that the only *minor* operation is one which is performed on somebody else.

4) To get prompt attention in the Emergency Department (even if you only have a cut finger): As you register, clutch your chest, say, "This heart pain is just killing me," then stop breathing until you turn blue. Service will be prompt.

5) Don't insult your nurse — she *will* get even.

Medical
Quotes of Note

The doctor must have at his command a ready wit, as
   dourness is repulsive both to the healthy and the sick.
          — HIPPOCRATES 460 – 377 BC

A merry heart doeth good like a medicine.
          — THE BIBLE – PROVERBS

He's the best physician who knows the worthlessness of
   most medicines.
          — BENJAMIN FRANKLIN 1706 – 1790

It takes a wise doctor to know when not to prescribe
   medicine.
          —BALTASAR GRACIAN 1642

I wonder why ye can always read a doctor's bill and ye
   niver can read his purscription.
          —FINLEY PETER DUNNE 1867 – 1936

Some people think doctors can put scrambled eggs back
   into the shell.
          —CANFIELD

Let no one suppose that the words doctor and patient can
   disguise from the parties the fact that they are employer and employee.
          —GEORGE BERNARD SHAW 1913

They do certainly give very strange and new-fangled
   names to diseases.
         —PLATO 427-327 BC

Good medicine always tastes bitter.
         —CONFUCIUS 551 – 479 BC

Better to hunt in fields for health unbought,
Than fee the doctor for a nauseous draught.
The wise, for cure, on exercise depend;
God never made his work, for man to mend.
         —JOHN DRYDEN 1631 – 1700

Those who think they have not time for bodily exercise
   will sooner or later have to find time for illness.
         —EDWARD STANLEY 1826 – 1893

When meditating over a disease, I never think of finding
   a remedy for it, but, instead, a means of preventing it.
         —LOUIS PASTEUR 1882 – 1895

The physician is only nature's assistant.
         —CLAUDIUS GALEN 130 – 200

Time is the great physician.
         —BENJAMIN DISRAELI 1804 – 1881

Health is better than wealth. Nay – health is wealth!
         —BUNDINI, MD

No man is more worthy of esteem than a physician who
   exercises his art with caution and gives equal attention to the rich and the poor.
         —VOLTAIRE 1694 – 1778

About the Author

Peter Meyer, MD, physician and writer, resides with his family in Wilmington, North Carolina.

The author is a graduate of Miami (Ohio) University, where he received a Bachelor of Arts degree in zoology and was elected to Phi Beta Kappa.

Meyer was unable to gain entrance into veterinary medicine school, so he pursued human medicine instead. In 1978, Meyer received his Doctor of Medicine degree from the Ohio State University, where he was elected to Alpha Omega Alpha.

The author completed a three-year residency in internal medicine at the Bowman-Gray School of Medicine in Winston-Salem, North Carolina. For the past 13 years, he has practiced emergency medicine. Dr. Meyer is a board-certified emergency medicine physician and a fellow in the American College of Emergency Physicians.

Meyer is also a successful writer and publisher. He is the author of *Nature Guide to the Carolina Coast*, a widely-acclaimed book about the environment and common animals of the Carolina coast.

Aside from medicine and writing, Meyer enjoys reading, running, photography, environmental concerns, scuba diving, and catching/preparing seafood.

The author's photograph appears on page 33, in the "Goosing Treatment" section.

Medicalese
A Humorous Medical Dictionary

can be ordered by mail.

Each book ordered by mail is signed
by the author.

Books can be *personalized*, too.
Print legibly the name of the person(s) to whom
the book is to be signed
(for example, "to Bob and Sally").

Order form

Send a check or money order only.

Name_____

Mailing address_____

City_____ State_____ Zip_____

Please send _____ copies of *Medicalese* at $ 9.95 _____

Shipping for the first book $ 1.50 _____

Shipping each additional book $ .50 _____

NC residents add tax per copy of $ .60 _____

TOTAL _____

Make checks payable to AVIAN-CETACEAN PRESS
Mail order to:
Avian-Cetacean Press, PO Box 4532, Wilmington NC 28406